Me and My Piano
Superscales

D1003188

Composed and edited by Fanny Waterman

Dear young pianist,

Would you like to play superscales? This book will show you how, step by step. (Our word 'scale' comes from the Latin word 'scala' which means 'step'.)

You will make many new friends here, including Cheeky Chimpanzee, Gurgling Goldfish, Dozy Donkey and Frisky Fox. With their help, you will soon be playing the scales of C major, G major, D major and F major. And you'll become a musical detective too!

When you play, always remember first to THINK, then to LISTEN (are you making the sounds that you want?) and then to CORRECT any mistakes. Practise the two notes in the brackets throughout to loosen up the thumb.

Have lots of fun with superscales!

FABER *ff* MUSIC

This book belongs to _____

I live at _____

_____

My teacher's name is _____

First published in 1996 by Faber Music Ltd.
This edition © 2009 by Faber Music Ltd.
Bloomsbury House 74–77 Great Russell Street London WC1B 3DA
Music setting by Jeanne Roberts
Illustrated by Julia Osorno
Cover design by Lydia Merrills-Ashcroft
Page design by Susan Clarke
Printed in England by Caligraving Ltd
All rights reserved

ISBN10: 0-571-53205-5
EAN13: 978-0-571-53205-6

To buy Faber Music publications or to find out about the full range of titles available
please contact your local music retailer or Faber Music sales enquiries:

Faber Music Ltd, Burnt Mill, Elizabeth Way, Harlow CM20 2HX
Tel: +44 (0) 1279 82 89 82   Fax: +44 (0) 1279 82 89 83
sales@fabermusic.com   fabermusic.com

Contents

C major
right hand

Under and over

Thumb under third finger going up.
Third finger over thumb going down.

C major scale

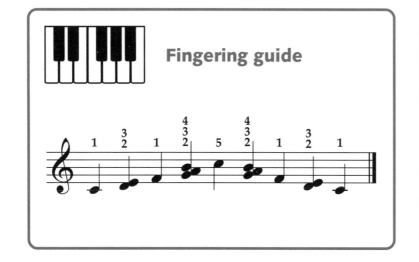

Fingering guide

Musical detective

Name the notes of the scale:

C __ __ __ __ __ __ __

Right-hand thumb plays ___ and ___

C major has: one sharp [ ]   ✓ or ✗

no sharps or flats [ ]

one flat [ ]

Chirpy chick

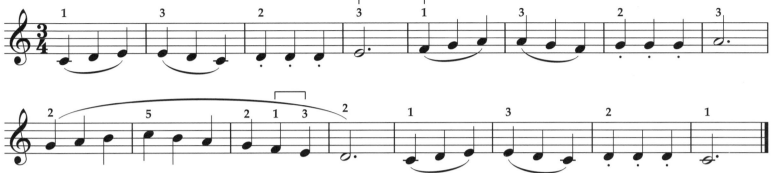

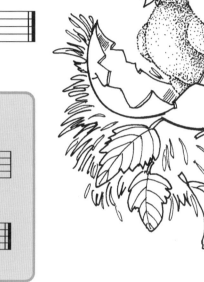

Accompaniment

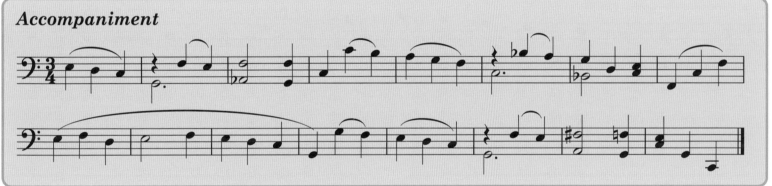

Cumulus clouds

Accompaniment

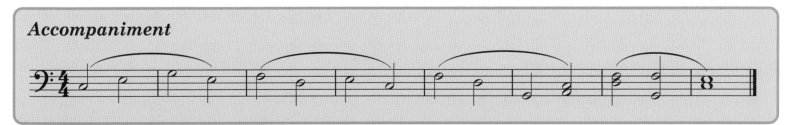

C major
left hand

Under and over

Third finger over thumb going up.
Thumb under third finger going down.

C major scale

Fingering guide

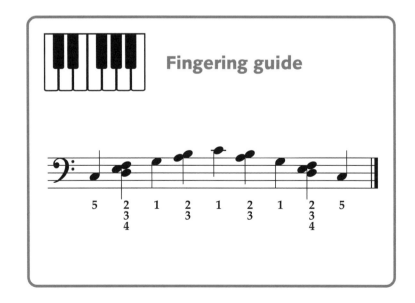

Musical detective

Left-hand thumb plays: F   ☐   ✓ or ✗

G   ☐

top C ☐

Add the missing note names:

___ ___ E ___ ___ ___ B ___

Curly caterpillar

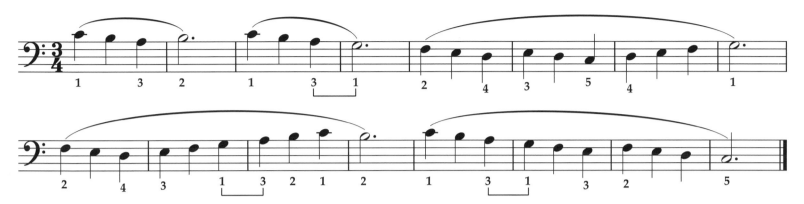

Accompaniment

Cheeky chimpanzee

Accompaniment

C major
hands together

Under and over

Use the pause to think ahead.

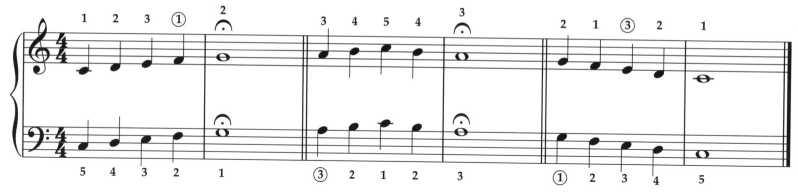

C major scale

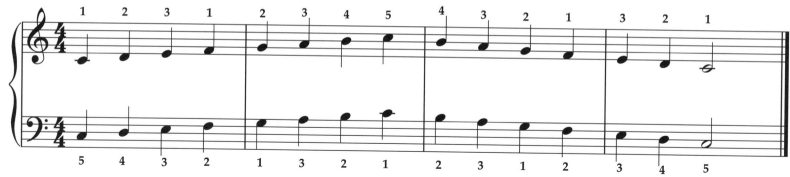

C major scale – contrary motion

Colouring the scales with dynamics

First play *legato*; then *staccato*.

Soft and loud

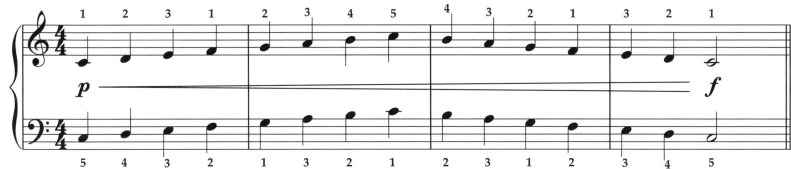

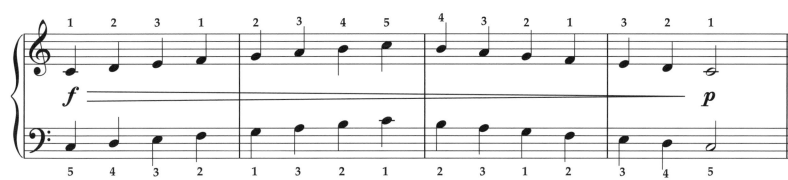

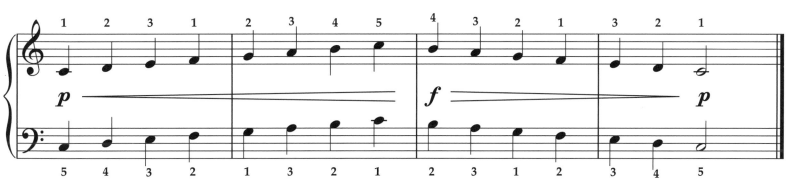

G major
right hand

Under and over

Thumb under third finger going up.
Third finger over thumb going down.

G major scale

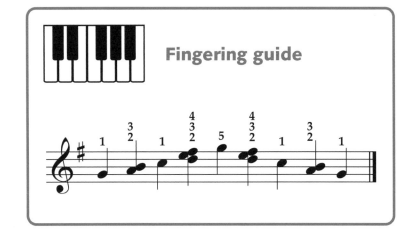

Fingering guide

Musical detective

G major has one sharp. The sharpened note is ___

Name the notes of the scale:

G ___ ___ ___ ___ ___ ___ ___

Right-hand thumb plays ___ and ___

Graceful glider

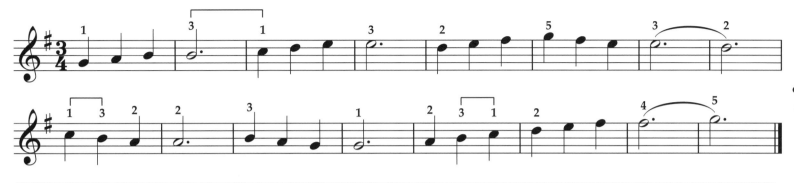

Accompaniment

Glinting glow-worm

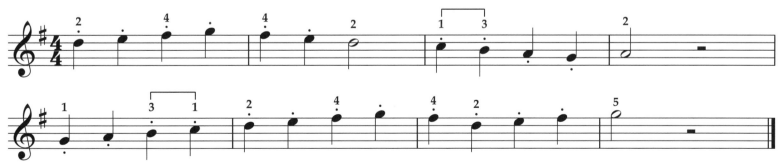

Accompaniment

G major
left hand

Under and over

Third finger over thumb going up.
Thumb under third finger going down.

G major scale

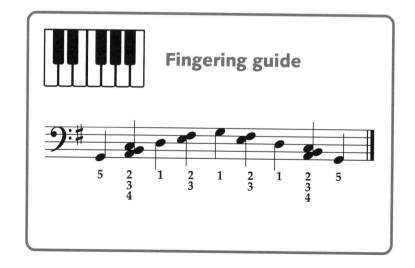

Fingering guide

Musical detective

Left-hand thumb plays ___ and ___

Write in the missing fingering:

5 _ _ _ _ _ _ 2 _

Gurgling goldfish

Write in the missing fingering.

Accompaniment

Grinning gorilla

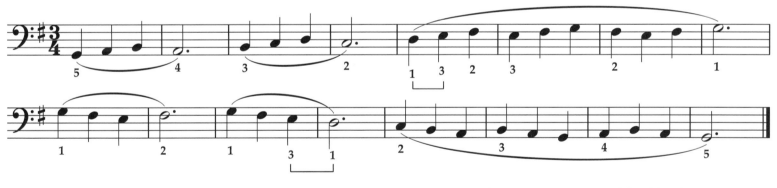

Accompaniment

G major
hands together

Under and over

Use the pause to think ahead.

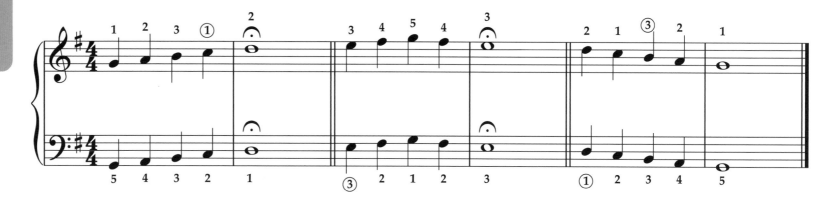

G major scale

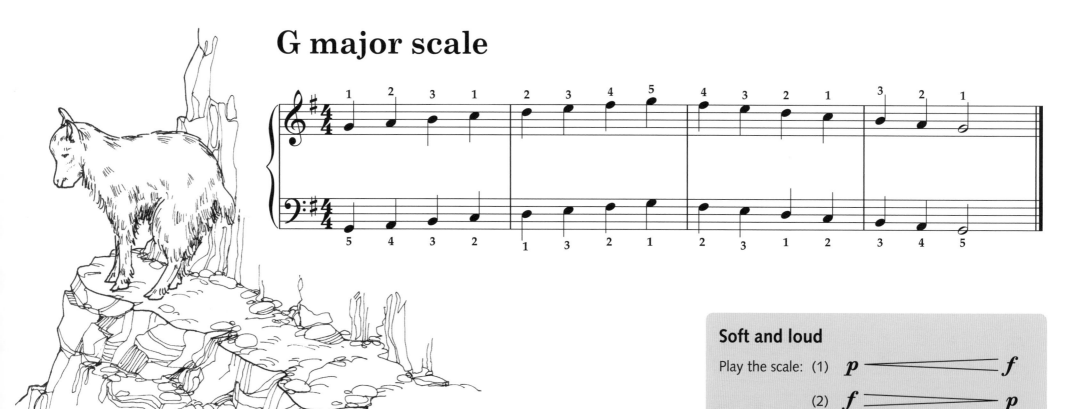

Soft and loud

Play the scale: (1) *p* ———— *f*

(2) *f* ———— *p*

(3) *p* ——— *f* ——— *p*

Under and over

Thumb under third finger going up.
Third finger over thumb going down.

D major
right hand

D major scale

Fingering guide

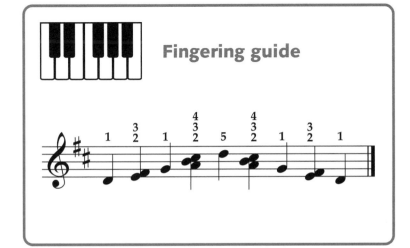

Musical detective

D major has two sharps.
The sharpened notes are ___ and ___

Name the notes of the scale:

D __ __ __ __ __ __ __

Right-hand thumb plays ___ and ___

Dozy donkey

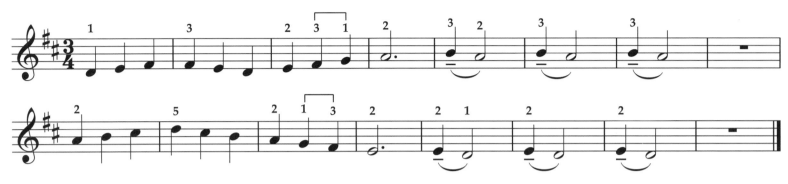

Accompaniment

Dizzy Di

Accompaniment

Under and over

Third finger over thumb going up.
Thumb under third finger going down.

D major
left hand

1 2 3 ① 2 1 ③ 2   1

3 2 1 ③ 2 3 ① 2   3

D major scale

5 4 3 2 1 3 2 1 2 3 1 2 3 4 5

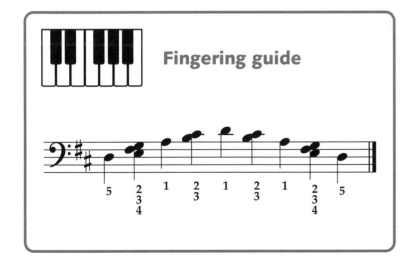

Fingering guide

5 2 1 2 1 2 1 2 5
  3 3   3   3
  4   4

Musical detective

Left-hand thumb plays ___ and ___

Write in the missing notes of the scale:

D E F# G A B C# D

Scaley pieces

Daring dolphin

Dancing dragon

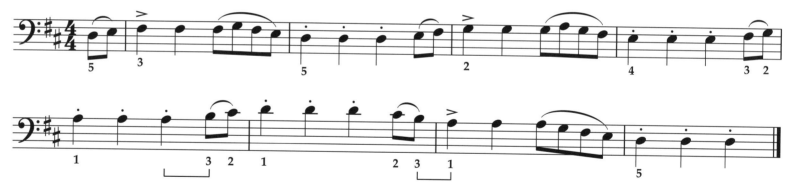

Under and over

Use the pause to think ahead.

D major
hands together

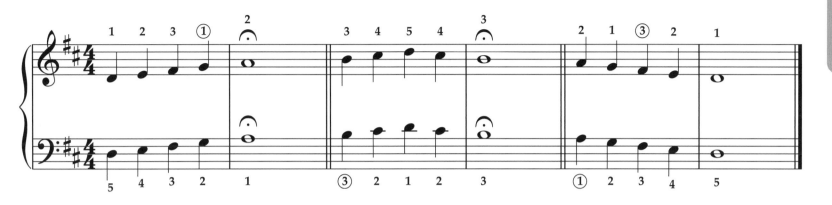

D major scale

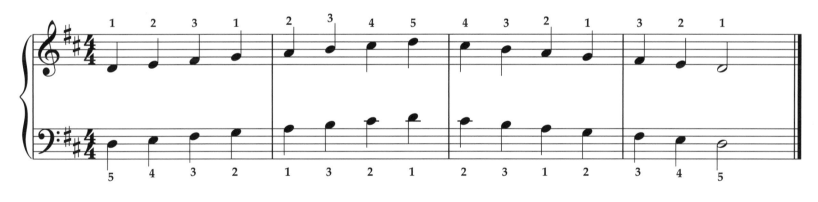

Soft and loud

Play the scale: (1) *p* ———————— *f*

(2) *f* ———————— *p*

(3) *p* ——— *f* ——— *p*

F major
right hand

Under and over

Thumb under fourth finger going up.
Fourth finger over thumb going down.

F major scale

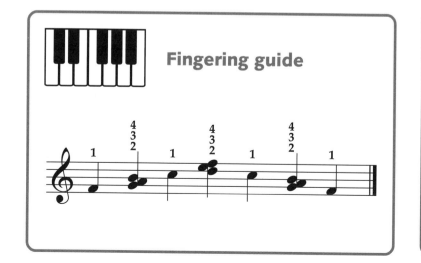

Fingering guide

Musical detective

F major has one flat. The flattened note is ___

Name the notes of the scale:

F ___ ___ ___ ___ ___ ___ ___

Right-hand thumb plays ___ and ___

Friendly frogs

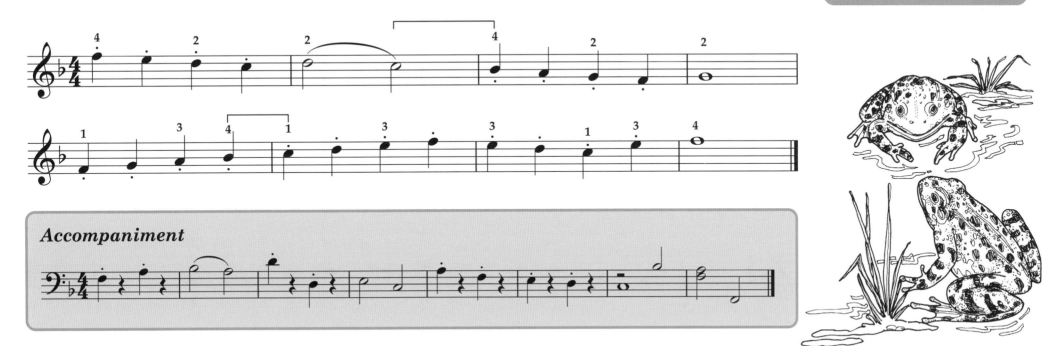

Accompaniment

Fluttering finches

Accompaniment

F major
left hand

Under and over

Third finger over thumb going up.
Thumb under third finger going down.

F major scale

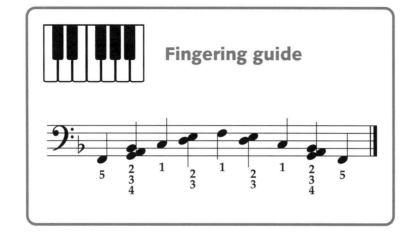

Fingering guide

Musical detective

Left-hand thumb plays ___ and ___

Add the missing note names:

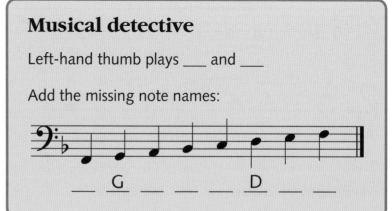

___ G ___ ___ ___ D ___ ___

Funfair

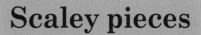

Accompaniment

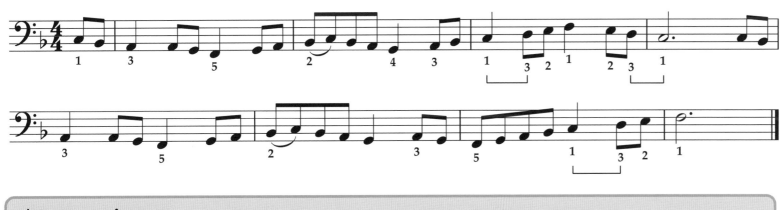

Frisky fox

Accompaniment

F major
hands together

Under and over

Use the pause to think ahead.

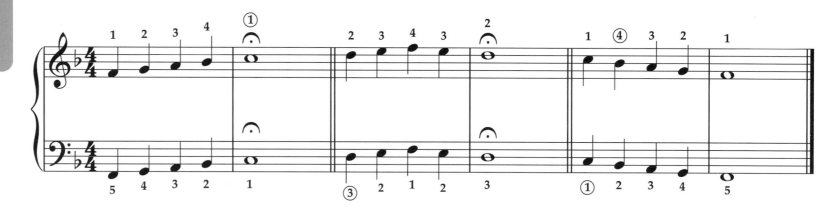

F major scale

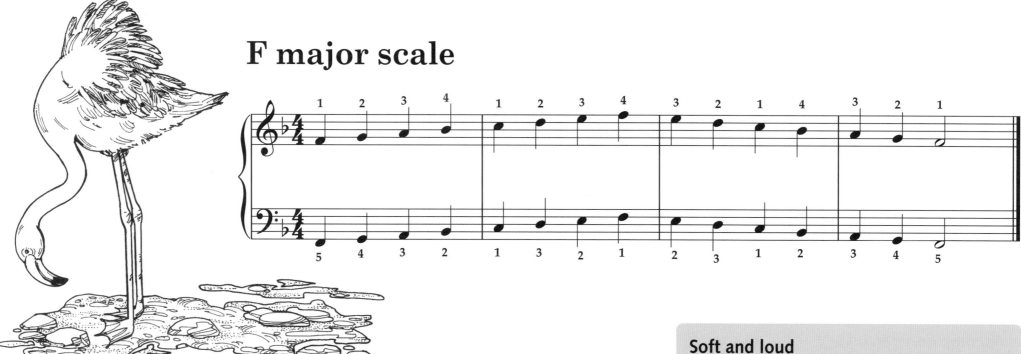

Soft and loud

Play the scale: (1) *p* ———— *f*

(2) *f* ———— *p*

(3) *p* —— *f* —— *p*